WISDOM

WRITTEN BY ELIZABETH WATERHOUSE
ARTISTIC DIRECTOR LORD R.E. TAYLOR

Published by Shadowlight Publishing
© 2024
Shadowlight Publishing reserves the rights to all written material within this publication. There will be no duplication without express written permission of Shadowlight Publishing or Elizabeth Waterhouse

ISBN: 978-1-7636761-6-9

Thank you Adonis for all the beautiful graphics. Either this book will be regarded as a book of wisdom or a sign of Lizzie's madness.

Hope it springs eternal
Though everything stays the same
Study human history
We're like moths to the flame.

To be ALIVE is a blessing not to be ignored
Remember you can overcome all obstacles
Growth is the acceptance of many defeats
Willing on barren ground to plant your seed
Always have a strong belief in yourself and others
With that you can overcome all of life's adversities
If your heart is pure and you wish no one harm
You will gain the happiness you so rightly deserve

Always observe the beauty around us
Rejoice in the sunlight, blue sky and clouds
Colourful flowers awakening at last
Filling the senses with joyful abandon
Colours splendidly dancing all around
Spreading such beauty and joy
Life bursting forth in sheer abundance

The world can be a beautiful place
But for some, it is not so heavenly
Where words can invade the heart
And destroy the contented spirit
Set it, questioning all it holds dear
Setting asunder all dreams and beliefs
Do not listen to words given in hate
Rise above it all and see your true worth
Let not jealousy or envy achieve their goal

They were so proud of all their possessions
Treasures found throughout the years
Unable to pay bills, all were taken away
Yet they still had each other to cling to
So, they picked up the pieces and started again
Never despair; there is always light at the end of the tunnel.

Life seems to be a revolving up and down
Days when your heart excitedly sings
Also, days when you feel fear and despair
When it seems there is no light ahead
Remember, all storms pass and the sun returns
So move out of the shadows and into the light
Change what can be changed to enrich your life
Accept what cannot and embrace each new day

In order to reach our desired goals in life
We sometimes stumble and make mistakes
All we can do is learn from these mistakes
And if we keep making the same mistakes
We deserve to pay the piper in the end.

We often give others good advise
Yet often we do not listen for ourselves
So wake-up and follow your own wise words
And always practice what you preach

One can soar upwards flying high with a great talent
And with grit and hard work try ones best to be recognized
But one needs no talent to be a fan of gifted people
Without Theo, Van Gogh may have thrown his paint brush away
One needs the believers, the teachers, the encouragers
For all types of talent in so many diversified areas
Science, The Arts, Politics, Health, Business, Technology
All doers and dreamers, needing support from their admirers
So always encourage, and applaud, you are needed so
Let not their talents be but dying voices in the wilderness.

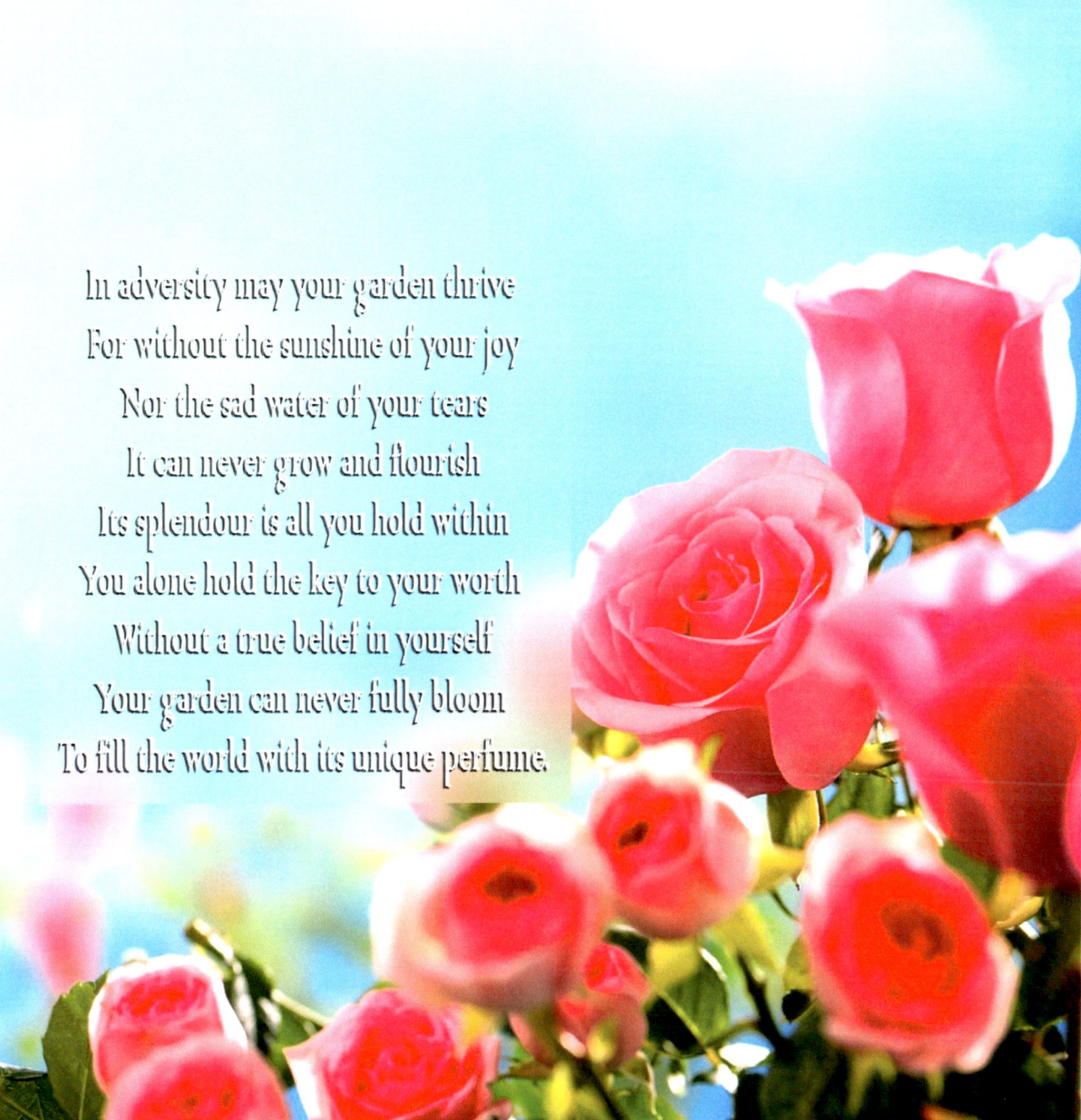

In adversity may your garden thrive
For without the sunshine of your joy
Nor the sad water of your tears
It can never grow and flourish
Its splendour is all you hold within
You alone hold the key to your worth
Without a true belief in yourself
Your garden can never fully bloom
To fill the world with its unique perfume.

Sing with the birds, sing your song
With your own special melody
Enriching the world
in your own individual way
Remember there can never be another you.

www.ingramcontent.com/pod-product-compliance
Lightning Source LLC
Chambersburg PA
CBRC091724070526
44585CB00008B/162